Thank you for using your library

The little book of table manners

Text and illustrations by Christine Coirault

for more books visit
www.frogillo.com/books

First published by Frogillo Books, 2005
copyright Frogillo Books 2005

ISBN
0954854829

Dinner's ready!

Be on time.

Ding!

Always wash your hands before every meal.

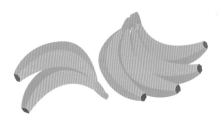

Wait until everyone is served before you start to eat.

No fussing,
no moaning,
but most
of all
no fidgeting!

Use your cutlery properly. Fork in one hand and knife in the other.

Use your knife to push food onto your fork.

Don't put
too much
food
in your
mouth
at once.

Don't speak with your mouth full...

...and do chew with your mouth closed.

Ask your neighbour
rather than reach
the

to pass something
across
table for it.

Keep your
elbows off
the table.

Use a napkin to wipe your mouth.

Don't play
with the cutlery.

Place your knife and fork together across the top of your plate when you have finished eating.

If you need
to leave
the table, ask

May I
be excused,
please?

Bye-bye

Goodbye for now!